Follow Your Heart

Book I

Finding Your Rhythm

By

Linda Kay Porlier

Order additional books at:
www.lindakayporlier.com

Follow Your Heart
Productions.com
P.O. Box 295
Leavenworth, WA 98826

This book is a work of fiction. Places, events, and situations in this story are purely fictional. Any resemblance to actual persons, living or dead, is coincidental.

ISBN: 1-4107-2425-5 (Paperback)
ISBN: 1-4107-2426-3 (Dust Jacket)

This book is printed on acid free paper.

Cover Design by Sara Pickering, Design Elements
Edited by Arleen Blackburn and Marilyn Crouch

1stBooks - rev. 03/12/03

Dedication

There are special people in everyone's life. These are mine.

Dr. Mary Martin Bacon, spiritual teacher and friend.

She gave me the will to live again.

Terry, my husband, for his unconditional love and constant support of my efforts.

Diana, my best friend and sister, who always knows the right thing to say.

Arleen and Marilyn, my new friends and confidants, who edited this book so it would ***soar***.

My audiences and clients, for allowing me to make a small contribution to the quality of their lives.

The reader, "May this book inspire you to ***Follow Your Heart***!"

Table of Contents

Introduction

When we look at a written musical score and see a bunch of notes on a piece of paper it may not mean much. But to hear those same notes being played moves us to a special place with special feelings. Oftentimes that feeling is so profound, it fills our heart with love, peace, or any number of other powerful emotions. It is not the actual musical notes as seen on a piece of paper, or even the sound of that music as it is playing, but rather, it's how that music makes us feel that motivates us to take action.

Many clients and workshop participants arrive looking for a new career thinking they are unhappy and unfulfilled with the work they are currently doing. But as we begin working, they quickly realize their discomfort with that particular part of their life is only a small portion of the whole.

They begin to realize what they are really hoping to gain is health, love and prosperity in all areas of their life.

People often think they want more material things like bigger houses and cars, so life will be easier. However, what they soon realize is, what they are really looking for is inner peace and happiness.

This is what I tell them, and am now telling you. Until you find your heart's rhythm, life will be a constant struggle and never truly fulfilling and happy. Life is not the musical notes on a piece of paper. Life is the feeling we get and the attitudes we develop as a result of hearing the musical notes being played.

Years ago, a nice lady named Pat came to me asking for help. Together we rediscovered her heart's rhythm and determined what career path would make her happy and provide her with all the material comforts she wanted and needed.

We began working through the process. At one point, it was Pat's turn to write her evaluations on the chart. Instead of writing on the chart as I had anticipated, she just stood there, like a statue. She had pen in hand, her back facing me; she was looking at the worksheet, but there was absolutely no movement in her body.

Not quite sure what was happening, I sat quietly for a few minutes. The room was totally silent. As the saying goes, "You could have heard a pin drop." A few moments passed before I very slowly asked, "Pat, are you alright?"

After a long pause and ever so slowly, she turned and looked at me, with huge crocodile tears streaming down her face.

Thinking to myself, oh-oh, what is going on here, I asked her what was happening. To my complete and total amazement this is what happened. Gasping for her next breath and struggling to get some semblance of control in her voice, she said, "This is the first time in my life I have felt as though I'm going to be doing something worthwhile and loving it. I actually have a reason to live again."

Oh, what this did to my heart! Pat helped me realize how important my work really is.

Years went by and one day I received a card from Pat thanking me for helping her realize how wonderful life can be. You see, when Pat came to me, she was fifty-one years old. Her kids were grown, gone from home, and she was single. She didn't know where she was going in life because she had always done things for other people and had never taken the time to explore and find her true self.

Well, that day she did! She was touched so deeply and profoundly by discovering her heart's rhythm, that she went out and made life happen. Along the way, she became extremely successful and had fun doing it. Pat realized that her career was just a mechanism, just like the musical notes on the page, to help bring about her heart's rhythm, that inner feeling.

In the years of working through this process with people, I have found they have what I like to call a ***biological clock*** constantly ticking inside of them. Every so often it sounds an alarm.

That alarm sounds when we are not living true to our heart's rhythm, and life seems uncomfortable. We may blame it on other people, places or things, but in reality it is our heart knocking on the door of our conscious mind, doing its best to tell us to get back on track and live according to the rhythm of our heart. Our heart wants that feeling of being alive and participating in life again.

Living according to our rhythm not only provides us with the material things of this world, but more importantly, happiness becomes a reality.

That alarm clock often gives us a warning in life. Usually, when we reach our mid thirties, early to mid forties, and early fifties, it tries to get us to wake up. Actually it goes back even further, back to our childhood.

How many times have you heard a child say what they want to be when they grow up? The parent, being concerned about their child's welfare, discourages the child from following their dream. So the child, trusting the parent is right, listens and becomes something they never wanted to become, believing it will make them financially secure throughout their life. All their life is based on what someone else believes.

Usually in the mid thirties, the alarm sounds again, and that child, now an adult, wonders what is missing in their life and why they are so unhappy. Please recognize that feelings of unhappiness won't be in just one area of life. It will be in many, if not all, areas of their life. And all of this happened because they didn't stay in tune with their own heart and follow its rhythm as a child. After all, they were told what they wanted to do in life wouldn't make them financially sound when they grew up. So now, at age thirty-whatever, they believe this to be true. Now they have a major psychological mountain to climb in order to touch the rhythm of their heart.

So, let's say this person continues on, unhappily, with their career. After all, mom and dad paid for their education. Now with their own children, or whatever reason they use, they maintain their routine and go back to sleep until the alarm sounds once again, trying to wake them up.

On average seven to ten years pass, and now this person is in their mid forties, and that annoying alarm clock goes off again! But they think to themselves, "I'm doing alright. I'll just keep hanging in there. I've done it this long so I can do it until I retire. Then I will be able to live my dream."

But it is interesting how little things and sometimes big things are seemingly going wrong. After all, with so many years of experience, things should be easier, shouldn't they? And why is it that they are so bored with not only their career but possibly other parts of their life as well?

Then come the "magical fifties." The body is changing and people feel so confused, often to a point of being distressed, and probably depressed, about what they want to do with the rest of their life. What is it they are supposed to be doing? What is it that will make them feel fulfilled and happy again?

Having come to realize they are no longer comfortable with the status quo, they know serious changes need to be made for health and happiness in their later years.

So you see, our heart is sending us messages throughout our lifetime. It's our responsibility to listen to what it is telling us and follow its rhythm. The younger we are, the easier the changes are.

This book is written for people of all ages who are hearing the alarm clock going off. It is for people who want to rediscover their rhythm and have the strength of courage to make it a reality in their life!

NOTES

A SEED THOUGHT:

"Listen - can you hear the rhythm of your heart?"

Linda Kay Porlier

NOTES

Ignite Your Fire

Before explaining what ***finding your rhythm*** means, it's important to explain how life works - actually how all living things are made. I call it "the fabric of life."

All living things are really a trilogy consisting of spirit, soul/mind, and body - now. Most people think that when they die they will become a spirit. Not true. Right now we are spirit and soul/mind, housed in a physical body so our true self is able to experience this physical world. Think of the body as a computer. In a perfect world, we tell the computer what to do and it does it. Computers also have programming that automatically makes them run. In the world of computers it is called an operating system.

We are built the same way. We tell our body what we want to do or think and it does it. Just like the computer, the body also has its own internal operating system that keeps it running. The body is programmed to keep things like our breathing and internal organs functioning automatically so we don't have to think about it.

However, when it comes to a specific, non-automatic action, we do have to think about it, and then take the necessary action to make the body perform.

The gift I would like to give each of you is the realization that we live as much or more in our spirit and soul/mind body as in our physical body, and that the physical body is a gift that has been given to us so that we have a home and are able to fully experience this physical world.

The spirit and soul/mind body never sleep, but the physical body does. The machine we use to experience the solidness of this world requires rest in order to continue functioning at its peak level.

So, having gone through that thought process, let me explain that when I refer to the heart, I am really talking about our spirit. The spirit and soul/mind have no boundaries, so they believe all things are possible and that the physical world has all the tools necessary to achieve any success.

The purpose of this book is to help us realize how much we are constantly communicating with our spirit and learn ways to recognize it.

By recognizing how the "fabric of life" works we are able to experience a happier, healthier, and more prosperous life. This book is designed to help rediscover and re-touch your heart and find its rhythm. It's designed to help rediscover that ***special spark*** to ignite the burning desire that motivates you to become everything you want to be. The physical body is merely the vehicle to make your dreams come true in this physical world. The spirit provides the energy and drives it.

It is extremely important that the body and spirit/mind are fed the right stuff, because one feeds the other.

Let's take a moment and examine this idea. When our body says it is hungry, we usually get a different feeling in our stomach. To be technical here, that is our hunger programming at work. So, let's say that vegetable soup is our selection of choice. What goes in that soup? Carrots, celery, water, salt, pepper, spices, onion and then it's cooked and eaten. It nourishes the body. Here's the point: there are a lot of different foods that go in the making of vegetable soup and they are all good, whole foods that will give the body proper nourishment.

We know that if we feed the body good food, it performs well. We also know that when we feed body improperly, it doesn't perform well.

And so the same is true when dealing with our spirit and soul/mind. When we do physical things like working or playing, it feels good. We tend to feel worthwhile and more self-confident because our spirit is also being fed. And so the more our spirit is fed good stuff, the stronger it becomes.

So in this experience of life, in order to live life fully and become everything we are meant to be, we have to drive all three areas of our being, the physical body, spirit, and soul/mind equally, and make sure they are being fed the best stuff.

A SEED THOUGHT:

"Good, better, best,

Never rest

Until good becomes better

And better best!"

Author Unknown

NOTES

When the trilogy is fed good stuff, it produces good stuff. When it is fed bad stuff, it spews out bad stuff. We hear it all the time in reference to computers, "garbage in - garbage out."

The purpose of this life is to become firmly grounded by bringing the head and the heart into balance. Only then can our life be fully happy.

All too often, people believe they should be totally spiritual - or totally physical. That just doesn't make sense if the goal is to experience and grow in this life.

By bringing the heart and the head into balance, we are also balancing our spiritual and physical world. Remember that our body is the mechanism for the spirit to experience this physical world so it can grow. Because of the sphere of existence we are living in, it necessarily requires that we live fully, within our entire self, to be happy, healthy and prosperous.

NOTES

A SEED THOUGHT:

"Today I am living fully in my whole self and creating greater balance between my heart and my head."

Linda Kay Porlier

NOTES

Creating dBest Winner

This is a book with an attitude - a different attitude!

Unlike most books, this one is not written with the attitude of fixing something that is wrong with you, but rather, it is written with the attitude of helping you discover what is ***right*** with you. It was written to help you tap into your innate talents and use them to bring about the lifestyle you are meant to be living.

By tapping into spirit, which for purposes here is also the heart's rhythm, life is lived from a position of complete strength and confidence and living life fully in its ***peak state***.

It is said that if you don't take control of your life, someone else will. When we are out of rhythm with our heart, we tend to allow other people to determine what direction our life will take. And the only result of buying into other's values and accepting them blindly as our own, is a profound discomfort with whom we have become and the situations confronting us in life.

So this book is all about creating balance between the heart and the head. It is all about bringing our ***full-self*** into alignment again.

Years ago, as I was sitting in a Psychology 101 class at the university, it became obvious to me that all the issues we were studying consisted of different types of mental illnesses. I hated it! All we studied were psychological problems and the different mental illnesses people could have. In other words, the focus was totally on the negative aspects of life. When I finished that class, it was one of the happiest days of my life. I didn't think I had learned what I had wanted, but as it turns out, I did.

Even though I was pretty young at the time, I had one of the greatest realizations of my life. In fact, I had no idea how profound this realization was until many years later. Each person has the ability to possess one or more of those mental disabilities and in most cases, if the person is willing, there is a way to overcome them.

Years later, I found myself working with a training organization that helped people focus on and develop their positive attitudes to bring out the best in themselves. They began realizing their positive traits and how to develop them into new, more productive attitudes.

I saw results that still astound me today!

That is when I realized how correct my college day realization was. Here I was, years later, watching these people change, right in front of my eyes because they were tapping into their strengths and developing a more positive attitude toward themselves and others. So, as it is with all things in life, it is important to focus on our positive and constructive behaviors, habits and attitudes to live a more productive and peace-filled life.

KEEPING AN OPEN MIND

When my husband and I were in our thirties, we had a business. By all standards, it was successful; but it seemed as though it was really hard work, and we were unhappy. The body, or our outer-self, was in good health, but the heart, that inner-self, was suffering. We had all the money we wanted and needed, but by our standards, life was hard and not a lot of fun.

So, we sold the business and had absolutely no idea what we wanted to do with the rest of our lives. We were looking for alternatives and started finding them almost immediately.

The key was that each of us had a positive attitude with an open-mind, so as opportunities presented themselves, we acknowledged and accept them. The result is that today each of us is successful in our own right. Additionally, we are both healthy and happy.

THIS BOOK IS ABOUT CHANGE

If you think there is more to life than what you are experiencing right now, this book is for you.

This book is about change – ***yours!***

If you are uncomfortable with life as it is currently, or questioning where your current lifestyle is taking you in the greater scheme of things, then this book is for you.

If you think you can use the ideas and concepts in this book to change someone else's life because you think they are off-track, this book is ***not*** for you.

Please take a moment and realize who is holding this book. It's you! And because of that simple reality, it must be your turn to stretch and grow.

This book is designed to help you realize how much more you can become. It is designed to uncover that unique and special person that is living in your heart.

I am always guarded when people or organizations say they have ***the way***. Please understand that this book is presented merely as ***a way*** to help you discover who you are in your heart and how you really want to be living life. But again, please let me make this perfectly clear, the contents of this book are merely to describe and discuss ***a way*** and is in no way meant to state or imply that it is the only way to find your destiny.

By developing a greater understanding of your true self, you will be able to build your own personal road map for life and become more confident and secure within yourself. How you choose to read this road map and experience your journey is entirely up to you.

NOTES

A SEED THOUGHT:

"Always keep an open mind and allow your greater good to find you. When it comes, accept it graciously and be thankful."

Linda Kay Porlier

NOTES

It's True Freedom

Friendship is the most wonderful gift life offers. And yet, at times, it can be so fragile. Often, friendship can be defined as the true freedom. When true friendship happens, life seems fun and easy. It's as though there is a certain energy that happens, making us feel good and wanting more.

When we become our own best friend, we feel the same way. Everyday is a new and exciting experience, and we begin to realize the qualities that make friendship so precious and just how important it is in our overall quality of life.

I like to call this ***respect,*** and if I had to begin to define it, it would go something like this:

- They (I) tell me the truth even when it hurts.
- They (I) listen and hear what I am saying.
- They are (I am) always kind.
- They are (I am) always positive/constructive.

- They give me (I give myself) useful feedback when I need it most.
- They are (I am) a spiritual being - religious beliefs are not important.
- They (I) follow the strength of their (my) convictions.
- They are (I am) a person of their (my) word.
- They (I) have good manners.
- They (I) allow me to be the person I choose to be.
- They (I) allow me to make my own mistakes.
- They (I) believe in 'what's right, not who's right'.
- They (I) always keep an open mind.
- They (I) willingly compromise when needed.
- They (I) know their (my) own values.
- They (I) have sincere strength of character.
- They (I) have high principles and live by them.
- They (I) have the confidence to follow through with their (my) decisions.

Sit back and take a good look at this list. It would be ever so nice if each person would begin thinking of themself as their own best friend. By incorporating these qualities in ourselves we can become our own best friend as well as someone else's.

Life becomes easier when be come our own best friend.

Think about this for a minute. When we really love someone in our life, let's say it's our spouse; we would want people to treat them with dignity and respect. And yet, when it comes to ourself, for some reason, we tend to accept a lesser behavior not only from others but also from ourself.

So let's make a pact right now to sincerely work on changing our self-talk and show ourself the respect we deserve. By more fully respecting ourself on the inside, people will begin treating us differently on the outside.

In Tai Chi there is a movement to dissipate a negative person or negative energy as it approaches. Simply take the right or left foot, whichever is appropriate at the time, step back while making a 90 degree turn, and move sideways allow the negative energy to pass by.

In this way, the negative energy is allowed to continue past, keeping all of that negativism to itself.

Looking at this in another way, we are not creating any bad karma. For years I have told myself to "take nothing and give nothing" in a negative situation. By doing this, we are allowing the other person to be the person they choose to be, and we also allow them to keep all the karma, good and bad, of their thoughts and actions totally for themself. This is an important element when choosing the necessary changes that will bring about more goodness and success in life.

By allowing the negative energy to pass by, rather than thinking there is a need to accept it or fight it, thereby wasting valuable time and energy, wonderful things will start happening. One of the products of this behavior will be that life seems much less stressful and a lot happier. Happiness begins each day when we wake up being as excited about living that day to its fullest, just as it was when we were children.

One more thought on handling negative experiences. When we become aware of being in the midst of a negative experience, it is our heart telling us that this particular choice is not in our best interest. It is helping us make the right decision for our good, rather than listening to others.

When my husband and I started dating forty years ago, everyone who knew us said the same thing, "They are the two least likely people to succeed in their relationship." Interestingly enough, we are the only two people that have succeeded in a relationship! Both of us agree, the reason it continues to be so successful is because we have listened to what our parents and peers said, discussed what we heard, and ultimately made the decision that was right for our relationship, not believing their ideas of what our relationship should be.

It's important that you do this for yourself too. Be kind and listen closely to what others say, making sure to have the best understanding of the discussion. Then go inside and have a serious talk with yourself. Then follow your own convictions. It is the only way you can be true to yourself.

That is self-confidence, and that is true freedom.

NOTES

A SEED THOUGHT:

"I am comfortable for other people to be the people they choose to be. If that is true, then I am comfortable for me to be the person I choose to be."

Linda Kay Porlier

NOTES

Plug Into Your Power

Have you ever heard it said that someone is living a lie?

Often someone is trying to justify their position for lying, by saying, "It was only a little, white lie and I only did it so it wouldn't hurt."

But when the other person finds out they have been lied to, how do you think they are going to feel? Betrayed! As a matter of fact, if they are rational, they will always remember who lied to them and will never completely trust that person again.

Once a lie is told, it has to continue in order to make the story seem credible. Soon everything becomes jumbled, and it is more difficult to remember what has been said and done. Too many things have become too distorted.

When I was in the sixth grade, I had been excused to go to the lavatory. The lavatory was located inside of the girl's playcourt where the school was stacking bundles of newspapers for a fundraiser.

Like any child, I saw those newspapers stacked up to the ceiling and just had to climb to the top. Everything was fine until I was almost at the top. I stepped on an unstable bundle of newspapers and down I went. When I tried to get up, my ankle was swelling and I couldn't walk.

I hobbled up the stairs and down the hallway to the nurse's office. I had a sprained my ankle. So the nurse called my mom to take me to the doctor.

Mom came and I was ready. On the way to the doctor, mom asked how it happened and I told her a lie - I don't even remember what I said.

Being filled with the wisdom that comes with parenting, she knew I was lying and told me so. I vehemently told her that I was telling her the truth.

I loved mom more than life itself. She was my world, and for her to say that I was lying crushed me. She knew exactly what she was doing.

That night I went to bed feeling terrible. I realized that I had just lied to the most important person in my life. So during the night I decided to tell mom the truth in the morning.

Morning came and breakfast time didn't work. So I decided that I would tell her as she drove me to school.

I tried - I really tried - but she told me that I would have to live with what I had told her and that she didn't want to hear anything else about it. So that was that, I thought!

A year and a half later, mom died and I never told her what had really happened.

What a wise woman! To this day, I will take whatever comes my way, but I will not, under any circumstance tell a lie.

The truth of the matter is, the only person hurt by any type of lie, big or small, is the person telling it. The ***mind*** is registering and remembering that lie and deciding whether or not it fits in our rhythm. Tell enough lies and don't listen to the message the heart is sending, and soon it just allows the lying to continue until it becomes painful enough that we decide to make a change.

This is how life works. Life is gentle with us. Life is soft. The heart speaks more softly than a whisper. You have to be paying attention to hear it.

When the gentle prodding is ignored enough times, the heart says, "OK, this is the way you want it, then I will be quiet and allow you to become the person that you choose to be."

Recently, I had an unkind experience happen. I found myself in the midst of a person who would do anything to have power, at least what she considered power.

I watched this person in amazement as she skillfully wove a careful web of lies involving other people who had allowed themselves to be drawn into the situation. I finally realized the situation was not worth my time or energy and just walked away.

While all of this was happening, it seemed painful, but when I realized I had been completely truthful and that the other person would just keep lying, I let go, just like my mom did.

Once I mentally and physically released the situation, allowing it to pass, I kept finding myself being happy again.

I made two interesting observations about myself with that situation. First, I never thought of lying to secure my position, and second, it became obvious that I was not keeping time with my heart's rhythm. Had the situation had been allowed to continue, I may have spent a lot of time being off track and unhappy.

Even though the experience hurt at the time, it turned out to be a major blessing.

So every situation - happy or sad - happens for a reason. ***Experiences are placed in our path, giving us the opportunity to stretch and grow.*** Years ago, I had a wonderful friend who taught me a lot about stretching and growing. Whenever a negative experience happened, she would say, "It's just another opportunity God has given me to create unconditional love in my life."

I like to call Life "The Great IS." Years ago, when I read Richard Bach's book, *Illusions* I noticed he used that term, and it has proven to be most helpful for growing through situations.

The great "IS" doesn't define experiences as good or bad. Experiences just are. It is our attitude that matters. In other words, it is our attitude toward the event happening before us and how we

are going to accept it that matters. It is a choice – a decision of the will.

Many people live in what is commonly called the blame frame mode. When something happens to them that seems uncomfortable, they always find someone or something else to blame. In their mind, it is always someone else's fault, never theirs. These people enjoy placing themselves in the ***victim role,*** and that is the attitude of a loser.

Winners, on the other hand, see the situation in the clearest light possible and then take the appropriate action to fix the problem.

Here are some attitudes of a winner.

THEY ARE ALWAYS KIND

There are times when we would rather do anything than be kind in a hurtful situation. And that is the time when it is most important to show kindness. Why? Simply because Universal Law states that for every action there is an equal and opposite reaction. It is also that thing called karma or cause and effect.

When we become agitated and want to strike out at a negative experience or person, we are bringing that same behavior back to us. Life is like a boomerang. When you throw a boomerang, it always comes back.

When we react to any given situation, it means there is an attitude inside us that need changing. It means there is a lesson to be learned and it is important to take quiet time and think about the situation. The quicker emotions are removed from the situation, the quicker we are able to stand back and see the event clearly.

Think about past experiences when similar situations have happened. By taking a look at the similarities of these experiences the lesson we need to learn becomes clear. Then it's just a matter of changing our thinking and eliminating whatever the behavior is that keeps bringing that same type of experience into our life.

When we react to a negative situation, we are out of control. In fact, we are allowing someone else to control our attitude and actions. No matter what is happening, remember that by showing kindness even in the most difficult situation, kindness will be the gift given back. It may not be at that particular moment, or from that person, it may come from an entirely different situation, but it will come.

THEY ARE ALWAYS POSITIVE

Everyone has met another person who for all intents and purposes, seems to be positive. But have you ever met someone who seemed positive but was totally negative? Sure, you have. And when they left, you wondered what had just happened because it felt as though something – not nice – had just taken place. Or maybe a situation happened that not only may have been embarrassing to you, but also the other people present.

All of us have had an experience like that at sometime in life. So here is a quick and easy way to recognize when you are in the company of a positive or negative person and that may include yourself from time to time. Ask yourself this question. Is this experience ***constructive*** for me and others, or is it ***destructive*** and tearing things, ideas, people, or situations down? By asking that question in every situation it soon becomes second nature to recognize what type of experience is happening.

By quietly asking yourself this simple question and watching the experiences unfold in front of you, the realization of ***what you want to be experiencing*** and ***what you have been experiencing*** becomes clear. When we change the situation we choose to participate in, the people that we choose to be around also changes. ***Winners do not choose to be around whiners!***

Years ago, I had the pleasure of listening to a great speaker named Skip Ross. His message was unforgettable. One of the major ideas he left with the group was this: When you find yourself in the midst of someone or something that you don't want to be a part of say this, "I love you, but I've got to go." Try this technique and watch yourself change. It is a fascinating study.

THEY GIVE CONSTRUCTIVE FEEDBACK

My best friend and I have an agreement. No matter what, we will always tell each other what is on our mind. And believe me, we have been tested over the years, but we are still best friends. We are still best friends because all of our conversations and actions are expressed in a total state of love. We know that truth always helps the other person grow stronger, even though at first glance it may seem difficult to hear. We recognize it as a growth opportunity, and only a true friend would talk that way.

For an instant it may be hurtful, but only for that moment. When the stinging stops and our feet are back underneath us, it becomes obvious they are just trying to help. Think how much more hurtful it would be if your best friend lied to you thinking it would help.

As long as the intent is spoken in a positive and constructive way, it is the truth and meant with love.

Friends should be challenging but at the same time - supportive. A true friend allows us to make our own mistakes, so we learn and grow and become the person we are meant to be. There are times, when the only answer is to walk away from a situation and allow self-learning to take place.

Friends are people to grow strong with you on life's journey!

THEY ARE SPIRITUAL

Now I am not talking about religion here. I am talking about being spiritual. Big difference! One is man's doctrine - religion; the other is God's love - spiritual. Words that best express being spiritual are: honest, sincere, open, respectful, reverent, and considerate, also at peace with self. These are just a few words, but please notice how each word establishes a constructive relationship with other people as well as ourselves.

THEY FOLLOW THE STRENGTH OF THEIR CONVICTIONS

It is not necessary to agree with everything your best friend says or does. It is, however, of paramount importance that you make a special effort to understand what they are saying and allow them to become the person they choose to be.

THEY ARE PEOPLE OF THEIR WORD

Have you ever known someone who made a promise and then didn't follow through with it? Sure you have. Everyone has. How did it make you feel? Did you wonder whether they still liked you? Did you want to know why they made that promise and then didn't keep it? It could be that they just forgot. But it is important to follow through when a promise is made.

THEY HAVE GOOD MANNERS

Having good manners will get us farther in life than just about anything else. Why? Good manners provide us with a track to run on. When we question how to best behave in any given situation, good manners will always get us through. Not because it is what is expected, but rather because it is the right thing to do. Remember, karma is always at work. It never sleeps. Good manners are always received well by others. They incorporate all the points mentioned above. Having consideration for others' good actions and feelings is important. Showing good manners means we are honest with ourself and everyone we meet.

THEY ALWAYS KEEP AN OPEN MIND

People who know their own mind have a sense of value. When a person knows their own mind, they are no longer afraid of what they hear or experience because they are comfortable with the person they are becoming. It makes it extremely difficult for other people to manipulate us when we have a sense of our values and know who we are and where we are going. ***That is self-confidence! That is success!***

THEY HAVE A SINCERE STRENGTH OF CHARACTER

This one only comes through self-honesty. When we establish high principles to live by, we will do whatever it takes to live by them so we can continue growing and developing our character. The question is never "who is right - but rather - what is right."

Take a moment and think about your best friend. Most people have at least one, placing them among the lucky in life. Now is the time to make a commitment to your self to be included on your best friend list. Why? You have to be your own best friend in order to grow a strong character and live a happy and fulfilled life.

To sum this up, it is all about listening to your heart and following it's rhythm to where it is leading you. That is what ***finding your rhythm*** is about.

NOTES

A SEED THOUGHT:

"Listen to your heart. It will never lie to you. It can't!"

Linda Kay Porlier

NOTES

Meet a Miracle

Miracles are happening all of the time. It's just that our normal awareness and attitude is not in that particular space at that particular moment.

A miracle is a common event that usually happens outside of our consciousness. So occasionally, when we become aware of something that seems to be out of the ordinary happening, it is called a miracle.

As we continue expanding our consciousness it will seem as though many more miracles are happening more often. In reality, it is only that we have opened up a new portion of our awareness, changed our attitude, and allowed the natural laws of the Universe to work just as they always have.

There is a natural rhythm to the Universe and each one of us has a part to play in it. So as we become more harmonious within ourself, we naturally become more in harmony with the Universe and life seems to happen more easily. Things that seem to have been beyond our reach are suddenly well within it. It seems as though it is a miracle, when in reality it is only that our consciousness has become more open and is allowing Universal Law to work through us. As we become more in tune with ourself, we cannot help but become more in tune with the Universe and how it operates. As a result, we are able to experience more periods of joy and happiness, prosperity and health, and so on.

But what about those uncomfortable experiences that happen in life? Each experience life offers, provides the means for us to learn how to make the right choices so we are able to keep our own personal rhythm. So when we have a bad experience, it is our heart telling us we are off track. Things will start to look as though they are falling apart with negative people and experiences, illness, depression, or any number of uncomfortable events and feelings. In reality, the heart is just trying to get our attention and make us listen. By listening to the heart and making good changes, it will seem as though miracles start happening. So is it a miracle or just the Universe letting us know when we are in harmony with it and living according to our personal rhythm?

Everyone has the potential of being a miracle and making a constructive contribution to Life. Our responsibility is to find out what our rhythm is and how to best live it.

Planet Earth contributes to the solar system. As it changes, so it brings about changes in the rest of the system. If one planet were to disappear, the system would change. If a new planet were to be born the system would change. Once again it is the flow of Life. It is constant and always flowing for the greater good.

Think about your body. There are a number of organs, all necessary for its proper functioning. The liver does one function, the stomach another, skin another, the brain another, the spine another and so on. Each part of the body is important to the overall mental and physical functioning of you.

Let's take an example. Every organ in the body has a part to play in the overall health of a person. Every organ allows life to flow through it and most often is able to repair itself as needed, provided the flow is constant and allowed to continue.

Keeping that flow going all of the time is really the only thing that Life requires of us. Stop and think about it, all of life is constantly moving. It is when the flow stops that life stops.

As long as we keep the flow moving with the rhythm of our heart, we will experience health, happiness, prosperity and the good things that life offers. It is when the heart's rhythm is cut off or stopped that our natural flow stops and problems arise.

That's why it is important to discover and recognize how your rhythm fits into the greater scheme of Life, or as author Richard Bach called it in his book *Illusions* – The "Great IS".

As we change, so the flow is automatically changed. As we change ourself, the world at large has to change because something is different. ***That is why one person does make a difference.***

When miracles happen, say thank you, recognize them as a confirmation that you are becoming more in tune with your rhythm, and becoming the person that you were always meant to be.

A SEED THOUGHT:

"Today I am contributing to the Universe with all of my being and I am happy."

Linda Kay Porlier

NOTES

The "Y" in the Road

Life is a series of choices. That is why the Universe has given each person the gift of free will. Those are the tools and the rules for playing this game of life. Every experience requires us to make a decision. And the choices we make determine what type of person we are becoming. Because of these simple Laws of the Universe, we will never be an ***end product***. We will always be somewhere on the production line of life!

I like to look at every situation in life as a "Y" in the road. With every situation we are given the opportunity to choose either the right or left side. So, no matter what choice we make, it is constantly contributing to the design of our life. If we don't know what the rhythm of our heart is, how can we know whether or not we are making the best choice for our future growth and happiness?

When we are making choices at random, life tends to become a jumble, pieces tend not to fit, and life becomes confusing. It usually causes us to become paralyzed at the juncture of the "Y". But please remember that life is all about flow; and even when we are standing still – we have actually made a decision – to go backward.

Life is constant. It is always the same, while at the same time different. It is the recognizable sameness with the constant and subtle differences that make this life so interesting and challenging. Everything in life drives us to develop our attitude. The attitude, whether positive or negative, is totally our choice.

I have a pair of cats. They are sisters born to the same litter. These two cats are as different as night and day. One is large and likes to sleep inside the house all day and the other one is small and wants to be outside hunting all day. The large cat sleeps with me every night, and the smaller cat would rather do anything than sleep with me at night. Both cats were raised the same way, so what is the difference?

The difference is that each cat has its own unique personality, individual design and destiny. Each one has a rhythm of its own. Just like a tree, or snowflake or human being. The law is Universal and it is the same for all forms of life. The Universal Law goes like this: ***No two living things are exactly alike***.

This book is not about discovering our sameness; it is about discovering our differences. It is about finding our rhythm and discovering that true essence, the unique talents that set us apart, and seeing them as being something good. This book is all about finding the person we are meant to be by touching that constant and consistent rhythm deep inside. Learning to listen to our heart's rhythm will help determine what our destiny is and how we want to get there.

So it is with every human being. We all have a specific and unique rhythm, and it is our responsibility to tap into it. When we get into harmony with the rhythm of our heart, life will be filled with joy and thanksgiving – ***all the time***.

For years people have been coming to hear me speak about ***finding your rhythm***. Many of them have given me the honor of helping them realize what their rhythm is and how they can best bring it into the reality of their daily life. These people have been my teachers, and there is one lesson I have learned from all of them. Each one has wanted to be happy, healthy, prosperous and loved. What these people have taught me is that when they were able to touch their heart, understand its rhythm, and follow its guidance, they became more at peace within themselves and subsequently became more at peace with the people around them. This peace is often called self-confidence.

Society has trained us to believe that self-worth is our job, how much money we make and how many possessions we have. So is it any wonder that we keep looking outside of ourselves, to the physical world, to provide our success? So if we should suddenly find ourself without a job, or not enjoying our work, or becoming over-stressed, or finding ourself depressed and not knowing why, it is nothing more than our heart trying to tell us that we are not following our rhythm. Our heart is doing its best to get our attention and help us realize that life is not working the way it is supposed to. It is trying to say that success is an inside job, and that no one else can do it for us. It is interesting how the really important things in life have to be obtained on our own.

Every person has something special to contribute to this world and when it happens, life is good. When it is not happening, life gets tough.

Earlier I mentioned the concept of cause and effect. I call it karma, and it is a sustained Law of the Universe. In other words, for every action, there is an equal and opposite reaction. As you give, so you shall receive. It has been said many ways in many languages and many different cultures.

Every decision made, whether conscious or unconscious, brings back an equal reaction. This simply means that when making the right decision for the right reason, good things happen. When we don't, we most likely will not like the results.

In other words, ***intent*** is the operative word in karma. If we give something only to receive something in return, chances are what we are hoping for will not be returned. The intent is wrong or we could say we have the wrong motive.

When we give with the purest intent and an open heart, only good things will come back. It may not be immediate, but it will come.

There are times when, because we are not following our rhythm but our actions were still done with an open-heart, it seems as though everything is bad. But by biding our time, goodness will be returned if indeed we made the decision with honest intent and an open heart.

It becomes really important for us to know the heart's rhythm, and know it so well, so that we are able to identify the signs along the way showing us when we are about to get off track. This book is designed to help you do that.

And yes, there will be those people who take our words or actions and twist them to the negative. But remember this! We have made our choice with honorable intent, and because other people are not comfortable with the people that they are, we cannot expect them to be comfortable with the people that we are becoming. So allow them to be the people they choose to be and move away from their negativity.

When we have gained the ability to tap into our own personal rhythm, we are able to find peace, harmony, and most of all, happiness.

While traveling in California years ago, I stopped at a quaint little restaurant and, of course, they had gifts for sale. I was moved to buy this beautiful saying, and today it sits on the wall above my desk:

A SEED THOUGHT:

"The fruit of the Spirit is love, joy, peace, patience, kindness, goodness, faithfulness, gentleness, and self-control."

Galatians 5:22

NOTES

Rediscovering Your Rhythm

Take a moment to find a pen or pencil and a writing tablet. For the next few chapters, you will need more than a small piece of paper. A personal notebook or diary would be perfect. Make it something you will keep.

Now, find yourself a space where no one can or will bother you. Some place that you can call your own - at least until you complete the following exercises.

Now, take your tablet, and at the top of it write these words:

Step 1: The purpose of this exercise is for me to rediscover and define my rhythm.

The purpose of this exercise is designed to help you rediscover the rhythm of your heart, that inner most part of your being where you feel safe and happy. It is also that place where you feel comfortable with yourself. In this exercise you will find the answer to that ***why*** question talked about in the previous chapter.

Now, write down the next heading that I have listed.

Step 2: My *Musts* Are:

A ***must*** is something that you absolutely have to have in your life to make you feel whole. It is a need that is beyond the physical body. It is what you ***must*** have in order to feel whole, complete and perfect.

Here's an example: Most people start with something like - I ***must*** have "time for myself." OK! That's a legitimate ***must***. Now write down why you consider it to be a ***must***. Most people would probably say something like - time to rejuvenate myself. So your first ***must*** might look like this:

Time for myself - for rejuvenation.

Now continue to list your ***musts***. While you are doing this exercise, please don't ask other people for ideas or help. Your ***musts*** should be yours alone. When you are developing the ***why*** of the ***must,*** it may be helpful to write down all of your thoughts and feelings to the best of your ability that have to do with each of your ***musts***. As best you are able, put your heart on paper. Write whatever comes in your mind. Don't worry about spelling or grammar or complete thoughts. The only thing that matters here is that you write down your inner dialogue.

Then when you finish defining each of your ***musts***, take some time; think about each one and explain the ***why*** in two or three words if possible. Actually, do not go over ten words for the ***why*** of the ***must*** because it will become confusing to your heart. When you get to that point, write it down on your ***must*** list. By the way, with all of the personal counseling sessions I have done with literally thousands of people, I have never found any two people with the same reason for having their particular ***must*** be a ***must***. Remember, no two people are exactly alike. Each person has come into this life with their own mission. That is why when you do this exercise, it has to be on your own. Do not number your ***musts***. There is no need for doing that right now.

Make sure what you are writing down are ***musts*** and not ***wants***. How much money you ***want*** to make per year is the only ***want*** allowed on this list. Other than that, no ***wants*** are allowed. In reality there are only about seven ***musts***. So you may start with a list that is pages long, but when you go back over your list and think about it, some items may fit under other items and other items may only be ***wants***. Be tough on yourself. ***This first step is extremely important in terms of determining what your individual rhythm is.*** This step is like building the foundation under a house. It must be strong, sure, and secure, so that the rest of the structure will be beautiful and sturdy.

Now, that you have listed your ***musts*** and whittled them down to size as listed above, it is time to rate them in order of their importance.

Now take your list of ***musts*** and draw a vertical line on the left side of the page. This doesn't require a lot of room, just enough to write a number. Please take a moment and look at the example.

Step 2: My Musts Are:

#	***Musts***
Ranking #	Time for myself – for rejuvenation
	List next must
	Continue listing each must in its separate box

Now, take your time; think about each ***must*** and make a decision as to which one is most important to you. To the left of that ***must*** put a #1. Continue down the list giving each one a numerical rating as to its importance to you. It is not unusual to rethink a ***must*** and change its number in terms of the rating, and that's OK. Just keep at it until you are comfortable with the sequence.

Remember, a ***must*** is something that you absolutely have to have in order to be the person you want to become. I often suggest to my clients that a ***must*** is something that is as important to them as the next breath they breathe.

Making a list of your ***musts*** may take a long time or a short time. Time doesn't matter in this exercise. What does matter is that you start talking to your heart and listening to what it is saying.

Here is an important point. The part about writing your ***musts*** down is really important because even though you think you will remember, you won't. It is also a great tool for future reference when you question whether or not you are living your heart's rhythm. I can guarantee there will be experiences and circumstances when you will find yourself questioning if you are making the right decision.

By doing this exercise and knowing what your inner most ***musts*** are, it will become much easier to make the right decision in life when faced with the "Y" in the road.

A SEED THOUGHT:

"Know yourself – it makes life a lot easier."

Linda Kay Porlier

NOTES

Assessing Your Assets

Taking a clean page in your tablet, write down the next step.

Step 3: My Strengths Are:

Now make a list of your ***strengths***. Many of my clients have a problem here, so to help with completing this step, I am going to provide you with some guidelines that have been a tremendous help to many of my clients in the past.

First, on your own, come up with at least fifteen ***strengths*** that you know you possess. That means just sitting down, not talking to anyone else, and writing down what you consider to be your greatest ***strengths***. In other words, define your greatest confidence in yourself and how you can ***offer it to*** or ***share it with*** others. It is important to take the time and determine your ***strengths*** by digging deep.

To do this, find a quiet place where you will not be bothered by kids, pets, television, or the radio. This should be just quiet time. Now listen to what your heart is saying and write it down. Just listen and write, don't judge it.

When the internal dialogue starts, get a tablet and pen and write it down. Please avoid the mistakes that I have made in my past. Everything seems clear and obvious when I receive it, so I thought I would never forget it. Wrong! I have lost some of my best input by doing that. So now when I go into the quiet of my heart, I just take pen and paper with me and write it down. Write until you are dry and cannot think of anything else to write. If it takes an hour or more to come up with these fifteen strengths, that is good. Just keep writing.

When you hear words or have feelings, write them down as best you can. If you see pictures - paint that picture in words. If you want to, you can draw the picture. However, over the years I have found that by drawing the picture on the page, it is always best to write the words you get along with the picture on the same page.

Once these writings are completed, take time to study what you have written. Then using the template that follows do just as you did with your ***musts*** and write down the most powerful, shortened version you are able to in the larger column on the right of the page. Continue on until you have your fifteen or more ***strengths.***

Now, on the left side of the page, just as you did with your ***musts,*** rank each ***strength*** according to its power and importance to you. In other words, what do you consider your greatest ***strength*** to be? Take your time. This is important.

Step 3: My Strengths Are:

Rank	***Strengths***

Here is an example:

Client:

- Intelligent
- loving
- good health
- ambitious

- spiritual - depth of character
- compassionate
- fair
- fun
- good communicator
- friendly
- take charge
- organized
- good computer skills
- good mom
- good wife
- good housekeeper
- good cook
- like to learn
- enjoy meeting people
- dependable
- good friend
- good driver

- like change
- dedicated employee
- hard working
- focused on task at hand
- good money manager
- enjoy change
- like challenges
- sense of humor
- analytical
- lots of common sense
- enjoy routine
- caring
- responsible
- independent
- enjoy nice things
- theater, dance, ballet, classical music
- like to read
- truthful

- honest
- responsible pet owner
- like myself
- enjoy learning about myself
- feminine
- open minded
- happy
- financially responsible
- intuitive
- Mariners fan
- kind
- like to work
- enjoy quiet time

Now for your second step, make another chart just like the one above, and be sure to keep it blank. Find a trusted friend, someone who is constructive and has your best interest at heart. You are looking for input that will help you build stronger faith in yourself and your abilities. Other people always see you differently than you see yourself. So this portion of the process is important.

Have them tell you the ***strengths*** they see in you and have them explain as many of these ***strengths*** as possible. Then ask them to tell you what they believe to be your greatest ***strength***. Be sure to do the **ranking** in the column on the left of the chart, just as you did on your own chart. The difference is, this time have your friend do the **ranking**.

It is pretty normal to be a bit confused or stunned when they say what they consider your greatest asset to be. After all, you most likely don't see yourself as being the way they are describing you. But this is important because this is how other people see you. Of course, you are writing all of this down. Have them give explanations and examples of times when they saw, heard or somehow experienced you using these assets.

Create a picture in your mind of what they are telling you. When you are missing pieces to the puzzle, ask for more input. You are not looking for the friend to tell you how great you are or stroke your ego. What you are looking for and developing are the ***strengths*** necessary for you to make the changes in your life that will put you back into your rhythm.

Now, find another friend or family member, but don't tell them that you have spoken to anyone else, and repeat the steps as described above.

It is going to take some digging to come up with these ***strengths*** but I guarantee you the results are well worth the time and effort.

This step in the process is just as vital as all of the rest of them. You will see why a little later in the program.

Let me give you an example of some of the ***strengths*** others have come up with. This list of ***strengths*** is from the same client. You can see how many trusted friends she found and the results are amazing. You will learn a lot about yourself by doing this process.

Friend:

- determination
- commitment
- conscientious
- dedicated
- very good mother

- seeking your own growth with diligence
- clear and direct communication
- good written communications
- seeks higher awareness
- focused on creating order
- create order through kindness and caring
- open to spiritual growth
- committed to being healthy
- dedicated to well-being of her children
- desires justice and well-being in the world
- has good friends/develops them
- loyal to her friends
- committed to material success with personal integrity
- manages boundaries constructively
- is clear headed and practical

Husband:

- good wife
- good mother

- good friend
- loving
- efficient
- courteous of others
- smart
- compassionate
- neat and tidy
- caring
- prompt and punctual
- thorough
- generous to others

Friend:

- loyal
- generous
- searching
- ambitious
- listener
- understanding

- insightful
- helpful
- intelligent
- loving
- concept-minded
- inquisitive
- direct
- fun
- thoughtful
- great laugh
- logical
- appreciative
- intuitive
- wise
- honest
- cheerful
- flexible
- non-judgmental
- humble

Son:

- intelligent
- compassionate
- loyal
- honest
- dependable
- hardworking
- persistent
- kind
- thoughtful
- open-minded
- good sense of humor
- realistic
- good listener
- generous
- inquisitive
- considerate
- supportive

Here is this client's comment at the end. ***What a great list!!!***

I have to agree. This list is incredible, and knowing her as I do, it is 100% accurate.

I can tell you, she was on 'cloud 9' for days, weeks and even longer. And the best part is she can humbly take ownership of each one of these ***strengths***. What a neat lady!

Now, take all of the ***strengths*** you have accumulated to this point, and again, find a quiet place free from distraction. Slowly begin examining the list. Then start asking yourself some questions. Here are a few questions to help you get started and believe me the rest will come.

1. Of all of the people who have helped with this list, what are the common ***strengths*** that everyone, including myself, believes I possess?
2. How important are these ***strengths*** to my advancement?
3. How can I use these ***strengths*** to advance myself?

Take your time and write everything you get down in your notebook.

Again taking the list of ***strengths***, determine which of them seem almost foreign to you. Ask why they seem foreign and follow the answer. Of course, as in everything else, write it down.

It is important to realize this exercise will require more than one sitting. But please keep this in mind. When you are sleeping, your heart is still awake and working. I always say that I like to sleep on an issue. More often than not I wake up in the morning with the answer that I am looking for, especially when I ask the question last thing before going to sleep the night before. I always listen to and write down what I get first thing in the morning upon waking and not rising. Once you are up, the chance of your listening, hearing and taking the time to understand the communication you are being given is slim. Make this a practice in your daily life and you will find that life becomes a lot easier. Keep it as a diary or journal.

When ideas start coming, write them down immediately.

Take your time. Don't rush through this exercise. It is important because you are designing your personal road map to live your heart's rhythm, which is the reason that you came into this life in the first place. By the time you finish this entire process, you will have a pretty good answer to **life's *big questions*** and that is – why am I here? – and - what is the purpose of my life?

People always ask me why I am constantly harping on this. Let me tell you a story.

A few months ago, I had the pleasure of judging a local queen's pageant. All of the judges had given up their weekend and took this honor very seriously. The competition consisted of ten high school ladies in their senior year.

As in any competition, the more we viewed and interviewed the contestants the more difficult it became to choose just one of them to be queen.

The chair for the event came into the judging room, formally introduced herself, and proceeded to explain how she had been chairing this event for the past five years and how this year would be her last. She had decided to retire and let someone else take the reigns.

Each judge was handed a notebook containing a picture and biographical sketch of each contestant. From this information we were to develop and ask questions of each contestant.

Studying the bio-sketch for each one and developing the interview questions, I suddenly noticed a young lady who had the same last name as the woman chairing the event. To say the least, I was more than a bit surprised and quickly found that, indeed, this young lady was the chairwoman's daughter.

Call me naïve, but I still didn't put two and two together. All I knew was that something didn't feel right.

Soon after receiving our notebooks and glancing through them, the judge next to me made a comment about how people always say these events are rigged. It was obvious that he was also feeling uncomfortable with the situation.

Well, we interviewed the daughter of the chair and I am here to tell you, she was nothing in particular. She just had standard, rehearsed answers that didn't really impress anyone.

There was another young lady who seemed to have nothing to offer during the interview. It turned out that her mother was a board member for the event.

When the judges finished interviewing all ten contestants, we were given a break while the pageant host prepared and served dinner to each judge with one or more of the contestants and their escorts at the table. We had the opportunity to appreciate these young women's and their escorts' table manners and their ability to hold a socially acceptable conversation throughout the dinner.

For the judges, this seemed to be the moment of truth.

When dinner was over, all of the judges were escorted to the competition for the public speaking, impromptu, and evening gown competition. Now we had the opportunity to look at all of these young ladies through new eyes and a new attitude to select the top participant.

A couple of these ladies were well-liked by all of the judges. Although not all of them were petite in size and not the prettiest on the outside, on the inside they were awesome. These young women knew who they were, where they were going, and how they were going to get there. They had visions that many of the other young women lacked. They may not have been the prettiest or the most petite, but they were definitely in tune with the rhythm of their heart.

The next thing that seemed unusual was how the judges were immediately dismissed at the end of the competition. When we asked how long it would be until the announcements were made, we were told at least one hour.

It was a cold, snowy night and some of the judges were not staying in the area and wanted to leave for the hour drive home. A couple of us were staying at the resort down the road and decided to stay until the queen and her two princesses were named.

Well, blow me over with a feather. Guess who won?

Yep-you got it! The daughter of the chair was crowned queen, and the two princesses were daughters of the other two board members.

But, here is the kicker.

It was obvious that the chair, the mom of the young woman who was crowned as queen, had been the chair for the past five years to be in the perfect position to make her daughter queen. It had also become obvious why she was resigning after this event.

If any of you moms or dads thinks that you are helping your daughter or son by pulling a stunt like this, let me be the first to tell you – ***You're not!***

Let me explain the ramifications of this situation.

First and foremost, now everyone in this small town knew for sure that the competition was rigged. To top it off, the chair has lost all of her credibility to ever do anything again with any school activity. And let me ask you - for what?

Second and most important, do you think she was really helping her daughter? I will give you a resounding ***no*** every time. What the mom was really saying to people in the community was, "My daughter is not bright enough, intelligent enough or strong-willed enough to win this competition on her own, so I will do it for her." The other thing she was saying was that at one time in her youth; she had always dreamed of becoming a queen and never followed through with it. So now she was living the experience through her daughter.

Wow! That is a sure way to make your child even weaker than she was before.

And third, the young woman who won this competition now has a hollow victory. Everyone will be talking about her behind her back and her confidence will be eroded even more.

What a mess!

How is this young woman going to have the confidence to make something of herself on her own?

If you are doing these kinds of things ***to*** your kids - my advice is ***STOP!*** You are injuring them. They must be allowed them to develop on their own into the beautiful people that they are meant to be.

Here is my point: When people have children, it is important to take on the ***responsibility*** of becoming the best that you can be. Children learn best by watching the people they love and admiring. As a parent, it is up to you to set the example. As a child, it is their responsibility to learn by watching.

Each person has their own individual rhythm or destiny and it is not a good thing to try to shape another person's destiny for them. What normally happens is the child loses their rhythm and then wonders why their life is falling apart and unhappy, later in life.

I have never really figured it out. Is it that parents want their children to always need them? That isn't nice, if that is the case. Not only is the parent holding their child as hostage, but the parent is also living in the past and not allowing life to flow through them.

The most important lessons I have learned in life are: Know who you are, where you are going, and allow other people to become the person they are meant to be.

A SEED THOUGHT:

"Every strength has meaning and purpose helping bring about our heart's rhythm."

Linda Kay Porlier

NOTES

Going Places

Let's take a moment and look at where we have been.

By now you should have a completed list of ***musts*** and a completed list of ***strengths***. Each of your ***musts*** should be ranked somewhere between #1 and however many ***musts*** you have on your list with #1 being most important.

Now take a look at what you are currently doing in your life. This could be any area of your life, like your career, or a relationship, but for this exercise take only one area at a time. Most often people take their career first. It gives them a clearer idea of what they should be doing for a career, and a feeling and better understanding of what they are looking for in this overall process.

Everything in life has meaning and contributes to where we are today. Often clients think something done in the past has not been a worthwhile contribution to their overall life. That is simply not true because every experience has value and has made us the person we are today. Our responsibility is to recognize how each past experience and deed contributes to knowing ourself more fully, and how each adventure helped create a greater strength of our character. Only in this way are we able to move forward with life and allow our heart's rhythm to flow.

Let's say the area of life you are examining is your career. Take a clean sheet of paper, and along the top edge, begin by writing down:

Step 4: Possible Opportunities

Please see the template example.

Step 4: Possible Opportunities

Must #	**Current**	**Option 1**	**Option 2**	**Option 3**	**Option 4**
1	0 - 10	0 - 10			
2					
3					
4					
5					
6					
7					
8					
Total Score					

Column 1, located to the far left of the chart, is identified as **Musts #.** Place your ***must*** ranking number vertically down the column. In the example, I have listed a possible eight ***musts.*** You may have more or less. Just list the number you have determined to be your ***musts.***

In the second column, listed as **Current**, write down your current career. Give each ***must*** a value of between 0 and 10, 10 being having it all and 0 if it doesn't fill your requirement of that ***must*** at all.

In the third column listed as **Option 1**, list a possible career that you may have previously or are currently considering. Thinking about each ***must,*** rate each one between 0 and 10.

Continue on across the page making a column for each career **option** and do the numerical evaluation (0-10) for each ***must*** just as you did for your current job.

Now add up the **total score** column. My example has a possible 80 points (10 X **Must #).** If the **total score** in my example is less than 65 to 70, it would definitely require a change. If it is more than 70, it would be good to take a closer look and think about what could and should be different to make it a higher score. This would require possibly reconsidering your ***must*** ranking number or view of what the ***must*** means to you.

When you have completed this part of the step, figure a **total score** for each **option**. If you have eight ***musts*** the highest possible score any one of the **options** could get, as in my example, would be 80 points. If you have seven **musts** the highest possible score would be 70, and so on.

The next step will take some real soul searching on your part. Study the chart you have created and see what each **option** will and will not do for your heart's rhythm. This part of the step takes some serious thought. If the **total score** is more than 10 points less than the possible highest total, you should take a closer look at it and see what it is that is not attractive to you. Remember, these are your ***musts***, the things that spark and ignite that flame in your heart.

Obviously, the **option** that gets the highest score is the one that you will most likely go with. But consider it carefully, remembering why the ranking of the ***musts*** is so important. If one of the best **options** has a big "hole in it" in terms of your number 1 or number 2 ***must,*** you may want to reconsider it.

Because this step of the process involves a number of different facets, I will give you an example of what your chart could look like.

Step 4: Possible Opportunities

Must #	Current	Option 1	Option 2	Option 3	Option 4
1	5	6	8	2	10
2	3	8	9	5	7
3	6	10	9	7	7
4	2	8	9	6	10
5	1	3	7	5	9
6	6	9	10	7	7
7	2	1	9	10	3
8	4	10	10	7	10
Total	29	57	71	49	63

By looking at the example provided, **option 2** comes closest to the perfect score of 80 points. None of the rest of the **options** even comes close. So if I were working with a client on a one-on-one basis, we would take a closer look at this **option** to determine what would have to be different to improve the **total score**. If there is nothing, we would look at a similar career **option** that would somehow incorporate many of the same parameters.

Once you have made your choice, take a 3x5 card and write down your list of ***musts.*** Carry it with you all the time. It is not wise to share this list with anyone else because they won't understand. Another reason you don't want to share your ***musts*** with someone else is because if they are not working for your highest good, they can use this information to manipulate you and that is not a good thing.

Now, when a future situation, job opportunity, or relationship, presents itself, pull out your 3x5 card and start rating each of your ***musts*** and how it fits into your life. Remember, when you rate each **must** between 0 – 10 if the **total score** is not 70 points or higher, as my example would require, it is not for you.

Don't even think about trying to change the situation. It most likely will not happen, and then again, is it even your place to consider that as an option? There are so many opportunities coming to us all the time that there is no good reason to waste time trying to make something work, especially when you know it's not right. And remember, it is your heart saying that this "whatever or whomever" doesn't fit with your rhythm.

Now you have a track to run on. You should find it interesting how things that have been a part of your life and have been challenging are not supposed to be there. It should become extremely obvious to you. The more different opportunities you put up against your ***must*** list, the better you will become at recognizing what does and does not fit in your rhythm because you are constantly gaining a greater insight into who you really are and where you are going in life.

Let's say it is your career. You don't like it because it isn't getting you where you want to be, or it isn't getting you what you want in life and you are just plain unhappy. Begin considering other types of careers that you might enjoy and rate them against your ***must*** list. Another possibility is to take a look at your current career and figure out changes you can make in it to have it fill your rhythm.

Often, when working with clients, it is interesting how often a life-long desire to do something surfaces and how, almost like magic, it will get a rating well within the range of the highest possible **total score**. If you have accomplished that with one of your options, that's the good news. Congratulations!

Now write a plan to make it happen. Remember, life is all about flow and change. So your plan will also flow and change. That is the reason why ***finding your rhythm*** is so important. It gives you a target to constantly aim for, no matter how many times that target may seem to move. Just keep at it. You will achieve your rhythm if you just ***keep on keepin' on.***

Now on the opposite side of the coin, it is always amazing how a person is able to come up with all types of excuses why it won't work for them.

Why is it, that when a person finds something they have always wanted to do they say it can't be done? Because somewhere along the line, deep inside, there is a major fear happening, and remember, we will do anything to avoid pain.

So in the next chapter, describing what fear is, how it works, and how to overcome it is the key issue discussed.

NOTES

A SEED THOUGHT:

"Know yourself."

Linda Kay Porlier

NOTES

The Double Edged Sword

Fear will either make you or break you! And it is your choice.

Fear is a natural response for any living thing - animals and plants, etc. Our solar plexus area, also known as the gut area, responds when we hear an unexpected loud noise or someone or something moves into our space. It could also be someone grabbing onto us, or slamming a door when we didn't know that someone else was there. This is our fight-or-flight response, and it is valuable and natural. In fact it is good that we have that natural, innate ability.

What is not natural is a constant fear of things that will most likely never happen in our lifetime, and yet we have a fear of it happening. Doesn't make sense, does it?

Or we have the fear of re-experiencing a prior painful experience. This is also common and the chances of that particular uncomfortable event ever happening again, are slim to none.

Think of life like this: Everyone is born in a mansion with all of the doors and windows open. The sun is shining through all the windows and even the hallways are lit with this beautiful sunlight.

Having an experience that causes pain, we run into a room, close and lock the door, vowing never to open it again. Why? Because we do not want to ever experience that kind of pain again. So we shove it down into our sub-consciousness (the room) and try to forget that it ever happened (lock the door). We decide that we don't need that room anyway; after all, we have a whole mansion of rooms.

Interestingly enough, as I was writing this chapter, I received a Christmas card from my sister and she related this story to me.

When we were very young, one Christmas Santa Claus came to our door. I was so excited, I was beside myself. Santa Claus has actually come to visit me! On the other hand, my older sister ran and hid in the study, closed and locked the door, and didn't come out until Santa Claus was gone.

As children, we physically try to close and lock that door to the room. But just as in that story of my sister, she had to open the door sooner or later, and of course did.

Life is the same way, there will be a time when that room we have locked ourself in becomes so uncomfortable that we have to unlock and open the door and come back out.

So life continues, and we have other experiences that are less than perfect and sometimes even painful. Each time we have an agonizing experience we run into another room and seal the door. Until one day, the only room left is the closet and it has no window or light bulb. And so we have successfully closed ourselves off from our mansion of life.

The only way to get those doors open and allow the sunlight to shine through the windows again is to open each one of the doors and face the fear behind it.

It becomes ultimately important to face those fears and overcome them. It is said that "face your fear, and it will disappear." Until we eliminate the fear holding us captive in that room, we are stuck and there is no flow in that area of life.

Psychologists have proven that a major reason for people being overweight is because they are trying to stuff down or cover up their feelings. These feelings are always connected to a fear. Until we face that fear we will continue to have similar life experiences occur and re-occur until we decide to overcome it. All or most of the doors in our mansion were probably closed because of the first painful experience we encountered, and the subsequent doors were closed in a constant attempt to keep that original pain hidden. The subsequent rooms were closed off in a continual effort to make the original painful experience disappear from our consciousness and that will never work.

In our attempt to keep that door locked, we find and establish an outer behavior pattern that other people will accept. Over time, the modified behavior will become injurious to our inner-self because it is not part of our natural rhythm. Do it enough times and we will get the same results as talked about earlier in the book on telling a lie. Eventually, we will lose track of whom and what we really are.

It is something that psychologists call a ***secondary gain***. Because we are getting a specific and predictable response from others by our behavior, we continue to do it.

Years ago, a business colleague and I were talking. She had excessive weight and for health reasons, she knew that she needed to get rid of it. She was stunningly beautiful and extremely intelligent. As a manager in a major corporation in a large city she was constantly outstripping the forecasted goals. So with all of these things seeming to be right, why was she so overweight?

When all was said and done, the reason she was overweight is because she was beautiful, and to top it off, had a beautifully shaped body. Because she didn't want to have the usual negative comments made about her and how she achieved her position, she gained excessive amounts of weight. So she did achieve her secondary gain of wanting to be acknowledged for her intelligence instead of her body.

The problem was that secondary gain was literally killing her.

After our discussion, she was able to get rid of her weight and today is still recognized for her intelligence, not her body, even though she is at her perfect weight and has held if for twenty years.

Everyone has a secondary gain. There are no exceptions.

When there is an experience and we feel the pain of it in our solar plexus and heart, we quickly make a decision to never experience that pain again. Everyone wants to live their life free from pain, but usually the decision we make at the moment of the event is the wrong decision.

It is normal to have these kinds of feelings. It is a part of each of us and our greater design. It is called self-preservation, and it is the strongest emotion we have.

But, when we over-react to this warning signal, we can get ourself into trouble. Let me give you another example.

Sue was a middle-aged woman who came to me through a newspaper advertisement to rent an apartment. She seemed nice enough and made a point of paying her money weeks before she planned on moving in.

The day she brought her money for the rental, she and my dog Kelly met and it was not a good thing! Kelly didn't like her, and as you can expect, the feeling was mutual.

Days went by. Sue would come daily and move a few things into the unit. One evening, Kelly went down to meet her, and she became fearful. She ran to her truck and drove away.

The next morning I received a call from Sue. She told me what she thought I should do to my dog. Instead of Sue facing the fear she had of dogs, she was trying to control him and everything else outside of her.

If that is the way you are living life, you will never be able to control anything. Until you are able to control yourself, life will always be a struggle. Try as you will, similar situations will get more difficult to deal with and you will just be spinning your wheels, making life even more uncomfortable and fearful than before. There will come a time, when those closed doors in your mansion will have to be opened.

I am sure that all of us have run into this type of person at some time. Parents, teachers, bosses, siblings, supposed friends, all types of people come and go in life and try to control what we do, where we go, who we go with, when we go, and so on.

The main reason for this book is to help people understand who they are, where they are going and how to get there. By knowing who we are, why we are, and where we are going, we can stop living lives of quiet desperation and do what we love to do. We will live the life we choose to live. The only way to reach that point in life is to get to know ourself and meet our fears head on. It is only in that way we will get the results from life we expect.

Here's the point of these stories. Both of these ladies were attempting, as best they could, to control everything in the world around them. The problem was that neither one of them was able to control their world inside.

Truly successful people are able to control their inner self. This is self-confidence. Being comfortable with who we are, so that we can be comfortable allowing other people to be the people they choose to be.

Everyone's mission in life is to find their true inner self. Another way of putting it is to say - ***touch your spirit, find your rhythm, love it and live it***.

We can attend every seminar and read every book on the subject and they can give us all kinds of ideas on how to be more confident in any situation. And they are all good ideas. But until we go inside, dig deep and keep peeling away the layers of fear that are holding us back, we will never have the self-confidence that our heart is yearning to feel. We will always be hiding in one of those rooms inside the mansion.

Overcome those fears and you will live life everyday, filled with joy and thanksgiving. All it takes is meeting fear, head on, every time one creeps up. Yes, this will take some soul searching, but the journey is well worth the reward!

I remember one year my husband and I went to Disneyland in Anaheim, California. One of the rides was supposed to be really scary. As we stood in line, there were signs all along the way that read, "If you are pregnant, you should not go on this ride. Exit here". Other signs talked about possible health problems that could negatively impact a person, so please exit.

By the time we got on the ride I was absolutely petrified. I did go on the ride but hung onto my husband's arm with all of my might. In fact, the next day, he had a perfect black-and-blue imprint of all four fingers, plus my thumb on his arm.

Not only was I embarrassed, I was angry at myself for getting so scared.

So a couple of years later, the next time we were in California, I made a point of going to Disneyland and going on that ride again.

Because I had gone into that room of the mansion and faced the underlying fear, I beat it. I had a great time on the ride the second time and it was difficult for me to believe that I had been afraid the first time.

The important point is that I searched out what that fear was and faced it. Once I did, it was gone. By facing my fear head on, I was prouder and more self-confident of the person I had become. I had just removed a ton of mental baggage and it felt great.

Most, if not all of us, have heard about comfort zones. Everyone has one. It is a fact of life. The mere fact that we are here means that we have a comfort zone. Our fears keep us from expanding our comfort zone because it may mean we will have to experience the pain of something unknown, and it could even be something that we are not able to control. Remember, we will do anything to avoid pain. And so life becomes boring, uneventful, and unhappy because we have cut off the flow by hiding in the room inside of our mansion.

Sooner or later the discomfort will become unbearable and we will have to face our fears.

Until we take a deep breath and make the decision to expand our comfort zone and are willing to experience any pain that it may cause, we will continue to lead the life we are currently leading; and if that is uncomfortable now, just give it time, it will only get worse. We are meant to be growing all the time in this life. There is never going to be a time when we will have all the answers, or know it all, or even have it all. Life isn't meant to be that way. Life is all about flowing with the rhythm.

The purpose of life is to build character. When we stop growing we are not building character.

So today, examine one of your fears and face it. The experience will bring such a feeling of relief, you will probably say something like this to yourself, "I feel like a ton has been lifted off my shoulders. I feel free and it feels good."

NOTES

A SEED THOUGHT:

"Fear knocked,

Faith answered,

And there was nobody there!"

Author Unknown

NOTES

Untie the Boat

Change is the keynote to progress. And yet statistics show that if you would take one hundred Americans today and follow them through life, here is what you would find. Five percent of people would welcome change and do it. Fifteen percent will accept change when required and eighty percent of the people would rather do anything than change.

So here is where we get back to the statistic of five percent of the people are successful. They are also successful because they realize that life is flow and necessitates change. They are so successful because they don't hang on to the past. They acknowledge what they have learned from an experience, make the necessary changes and move on. Life for them is constantly flowing.

So why is it that people hang onto their past? Is it because they fear the pain they might experience by moving forward? Or are they afraid that people won't like them anymore? Or is it that they fear they won't be as successful as they are right now?

Let's take a minute to answer each one of these questions. Why is it that people hang onto their past? For some reason, experiences always seem better when they are memories. The mind has a wonderful way of bringing light to sad or painful experiences. That is not to say they don't feel the pain of the loss of a loved one. But it does mean that all of the traumatic events leading up to the death have most likely softened through the years. So, in other words, we want to hang onto the memory of an experience that has happened in our past. Past is the key word here. If a loved one has passed, they will not pass again. It is already done. So, it is just the memory that is being clung to. It is important to put the past in the proper perspective so that the past is not confused with life today.

Is it because they fear the pain that a new experience may bring? Whenever life moves forward, something is left behind. It is one of those Universal Laws. That is why this book is so important. It becomes a personal guide to help us realize what is no longer important so that we can leave it behind. You know the old saying, "You cannot fit a camel through the eye of a needle." It can't be done.

Most people take the meaning of that quote at a purely materialistic level and don't have any understanding of what it means. Take another look at it from the psychological side. It will give you a whole new perspective on living life.

Too much baggage is really hard to carry. Oftentimes, when we move forward and leave something behind, psychologically or materially, it seems as though there will be a void in life. But remember that nature abhors a vacuum. Retired people usually become busier than they were when they were going to a daily job. When we get rid of a piece of furniture it is always replaced with something else. When we move forward and leave the past where it belongs, we will not be dropping off the face of the earth, we will only find more things and friends that are much more fulfilling to the direction we are going in life.

Or are they afraid that people won't like them anymore? This is most often one of the ***big ones*** for people. Listen carefully when I say this. If people no longer want to be a part of your life, then it means, the lesson they came to teach is done. They will not be a productive part of your new life, so let them go. It gets hard when it is family, but this is sometimes necessary too. Be sure when you let go, there are no hard feelings. Just allow them to be the people they choose to be. Life is all about change. Because of past training, many will have a hard time with that concept. But sometimes it is the very thing needed to be done with someone so we don't have to dance with that person ever again.

Show me one day that was exactly like today. Please point out one person that is exactly like another, a flower that is exactly the same as another, a sunset that is exactly like an earlier one. No two things in life are exactly the same. The reason for this is so that we will learn to accept, appreciate and grow with change. It doesn't have to be a radical change. It just has to be change - flow.

Are you afraid to move forward in life because you may not be as successful as you are right now? I remember having cheesecake at a small outdoor restaurant one day with my father. He had become very successful in his business but our relationship was not always the best. I remember dad looking at me and asking me how I would define success. To my amazement I answered him by saying,

"Success is a state of mind." We both sat there thinking about that comment for a long time.

Over the years, I have considered that comment a lot and have come to this conclusion. If it isn't fun, don't do it. And if it doesn't make you happy, don't do it. Life is constantly sending us enough experiences to help us learn and change. It is our attitude that is the key to fun and happiness. ***Fun and happiness are a choice and you get to choose!***

Abusers like to hang on. As a matter of fact, the more abusive they are, the more difficult it is for them to let go. Why? They can't let go, because they are scared to death of meeting their greatest fear. So don't be an abuser to yourself and don't allow other people to abuse you. Successful people meet their greatest fears and overcome them with poise and dignity. That is being true to your rhythm.

NOTES

A SEED THOUGHT:

"If you want to leave the dock - untie the boat."

Linda Kay Porlier

NOTES

It's Your Choice

Ralph Waldo Trine, author of *In Tune with the Infinite* wrote the following story in his book. It is one that I carry in my heart all of the time.

The story goes like this:

A gentle man lived in the country. On his property was a beautiful pond. The pond was fed its water through a gate from a reservoir higher up the hill on his property. It fed the pond and continued down the hillside as a beautiful creek.

The pond bloomed with the most beautiful water lilies in the spring and summer and around the pond were all kinds of flora and fauna, adding to the extraordinary beauty of the area. Around the pond were benches where people were able to come and "be". There were no signs saying, "no trespassing". The gate to this serene setting was always open and all were welcome.

As the creek flowed down the hill, along its sides were wild flowers that bloomed most of the year and grass that shown as a beautiful carpet of green. The cattle and horses and other creatures were able to partake of the life-nourishing, crystal clear, pure water that flowed under the fence onto their property. It was truly a pristine area.

One day the gentle man left for one year to work his business and rented his property to another man. The man went up the hill and turned off the water so it no longer ran through the gate that regulated the flow of the life-giving water into the pond.

Soon the beautiful water lilies lay dead on the bottom of the empty pond with their stems stretched and shriveled. The flora and fauna surrounding the pond died and became brown and ugly. The wild flowers were no more and the soft green carpet of grass was matted and dying.

The cattle and horses, that so needed the life-giving water to nourish their bodies, were gone.

And at last, the man closed the gate to the sitting area by the pond and no one was welcome. There would be no more "soothing for people's souls".

So, I ask you, which person do you want to be - the gentle man or the man filled with avarice? Do you want to flow with life-giving water or keep it only for yourself?

The choice is yours. You can only be one or the other. You cannot be both.

NOTES

A SEED THOUGHT:

"Life is yours to do with what you want. Make constructive choices."

Linda Kay Porlier

NOTES

HOME IS IN THE HEART

"There is a special place,

In each person's heart,

A place known as home.

When we reach it, we know it,

As a soft hush enters the soul.

Hush.

Be still,

And know why you are."

Linda Kay Porlier

NOTES

About the Author

Linda Kay Porlier, President of Follow Your Heart Productions, Inc. is a well-respected sales and communication consultant working with many of America's best companies. She has authored *S3-Selling Strategies and Solutions: Selling Your Way to Success* and *Management Communication Skills for Leaders.* In 1982 she developed a powerful process to help people and companies identify ***who they are, where they are going and how they are going to get***

there. Today, she continues to offer seminars, retreats and personal coaching for people and companies looking for ways to ***find their rhythm***. As an inspirational and motivational speaker she is in constant demand for conventions, retreats and corporate meetings. Listed in *Who's Who in the West* and *Who's Who of Emerging Leaders in America*, she has found her rhythm.

Printed in the United States
17521LVS00004B/1-96